GW00760454

What a Wonderful World!

Contents

Published by
CJ Fallon
Ground Floor – Block B
Liffey Valley Office Campus
Dublin 22

First Edition April 2010

©
Angela Griffin and Liz Sheehy

Illustrations by Geoff Ball

Acknowledgements
The publishers gratefully acknowledge the following for permission to reproduce copyright materials:
AKG London for the photograph of Thomas Edison; The Irish Historical Picture Company for the photograph of Shop Street.

Every effort has been made to secure permission to reproduce copyright material in this book. However, if the publishers have inadvertently overlooked any copyright holders, they will be pleased to come to a suitable arrangement with them at the earliest opportunity.

Printed in Ireland by
ColourBooks Limited
105 Baldoyle Industrial Estate
Baldoyle
Dublin 13

All about me!

Name: Adam

Address:

Phone number: 0860781069

This is my teacher.

This is my school.

These are my friends.

This is my home.

This is my family.

You as a baby

Find out all you can about when you were a baby.

When were you born? _traler_

Where were you born? _____

What weight were you? _____

Who did you look like? _nice_

Describe your hair. _black_

How old were you when you started to walk? _5_

The first word you said when
you were a baby was _____.

What did you drink? _milk_

What did you eat? _baby food_

_____

Where did you sleep? _in a cat_

What was your favourite toy? _Thomas_

Growing

Your body is growing all the time. When you were a baby, you had small bones. Now your bones are bigger and you can do more things. Think about how you have grown and changed.

This is something I used when I was a baby.

This is something I use now.

When I was a baby, I could not...

Write
run
Talk
Fall
read
Jump

Now I can do many things by myself.

At school, I can PLAY .

At home, I can dance .

With my friends, I can have fun .

When I am fully grown, I will be able to WaLK .

My family tree

People belong to families.
The people who belong to your family are called your relations.
Draw pictures of you and your relations in the family tree.

Cassandra

Nathan

Papa

Joseph

Fabian

Nana

Alanna

Ciara

Adam

me

What rot?

Find out what happens to different rubbish when it is buried.
You will need a large plastic box, soil, cling film and rubbish –
tea bags, newspaper, bread, crisp bag, drink carton and apple core.

1. Fill ¼ of the box with soil and put your rubbish on top.
2. Cover with more soil and dampen.
3. Cover the top of the box with cling film.
4. Put the box in a warm place.
5. After one week, empty the soil and rubbish on to a newspaper.
   Examine the rubbish. Fill in the chart below.
6. Put the soil and rubbish back into the box.
   Examine it after another week.

	my guess about what will happen	week 1	week 2
tea bag			
newspaper			
bread			
crisp bag			
drink carton			
apple core			

What have you learned about caring for your world?

A famous inventor

Thomas Edison enjoyed making things. He was born in America in 1847. He went to school only for a short time. His mother then taught him at home. As a boy, he did experiments in the basement of his house. When Edison was growing up, homes, schools and workplaces were much darker places than they are today. Candles and oil lamps were used to give light, but the light from these was very dim.

 Thomas Edison invented the electric light bulb and this made him famous. He also designed a system of power plants to bring electricity into people's homes.

Thomas Edison continued thinking up new ideas all his life. He was a very hard worker and only slept for six hours each night; the rest of the time he worked on his ideas.

He invented the phonograph. The phonograph was the first machine that could record the sound of someone's voice and play it back. He recited the nursery rhyme 'Mary had a little lamb' and the phonograph played the words back to him. Edison invented this even though his hearing was so poor he thought of himself as deaf.

He also invented a camera for showing films in a cinema. It was called the cine camera. Edison was called 'The Wizard' because by the time he died, he had made more than 3000 inventions.

The next time you switch on a light, think about the man who invented it!

Imagine you are an inventor.
Draw an invention.

Talk to your classmates about your ideas.

A (map) of my bedroom

Maps give you a bird's-eye view of places.
If you flew over your neighbourhood in an aeroplane,
you could see your house.
You could also see roads and buildings where you live.
A drawing of this is called a map.
Maps only show where important things are.
They do not show things that move about, like people or cars.
Kate made this map of her bedroom.

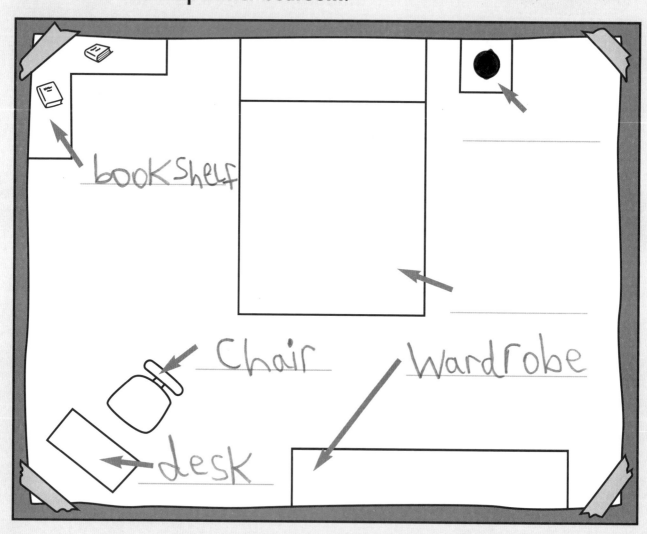

bookshelf

chair   wardrobe

desk

Label the furniture in the map. These words might help you.

bookshelf   desk   wardrobe   locker   bed   chair

Draw in a window and door.

A room with a view!

Make a map of a room in your house. An adult can help you.
Think about the shape of the room. Draw the four walls first.
Then put in the door, window and furniture. Lastly, add labels.
Don't forget…it's a bird's-eye view!

Autumn

Trees are covered with green leaves in summer. Leaves are like little factories. They make food for the trees. They need sunshine, water and air to make food. In autumn, the leaves of deciduous trees cannot make food anymore. They turn yellow, red,

 orange and brown. The leaves die and fall off the trees. Evergreen trees do not lose their leaves in autumn. The fir tree is an evergreen.

Answer these questions about autumn.

1. What colour do leaves turn in autumn?

   _____

2. What is the fruit of
   the oak tree? _____

   the horse chestnut tree? _____

3. Name the three months of autumn.

   _____   _____   _____

4. Name four fruits that are ripe in Ireland in autumn.

   (a) _____   (b) _____

   (c) _____   (d) _____

5. Name three hibernating animals.

   (a) _____   (b) _____   (c) _____

Science

The swallow

Swallows leave Ireland every autumn. They do not like our cold winters. They fly to South Africa where it is warmer. This journey takes six weeks and is called migration. Swallows fly through France, Spain and Morocco. Then they cross the Sahara Desert and the Congo rainforest. Finally, they reach South Africa.

Swallows migrate in daylight and can travel up to 320km each day. At night, they roost in huge flocks. They don't need to fatten up before their long journey as they snap up their food along the way. They only eat flying insects. Not all swallows survive the journey. Those that do, stay in South Africa until the end of February and then make their journey back to us. Many people see their return as a sign that summer is on its way.

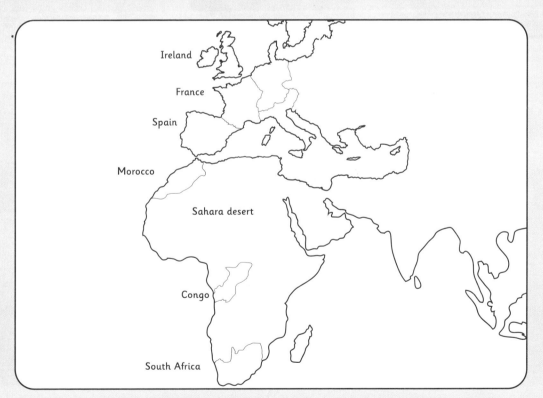

Draw a line to show the swallow's migration route.
Colour the land green and the seas blue.

Irish wildlife

The wild animals below live in Ireland.
Write the correct name under each picture.
Put a ✓ beside each animal you have seen.

mouse ✓ deer ✓ badger ✓ otter ✓ fox ✓ bat ✓
rabbit ✓ hare ✓ frog ✓ hedgehog ✓ seal ✓ squirrel ✓

rabbit ✓   Squirrel ✓   otter ✓

badger ✓   frog ✓   Mouse ✓

fox ✓   Seal ✗   deer ✓

bat ✓   hegehog ✓   hare ✓

What do plants need to grow?

Get four margarine tubs. Put cotton wool in each and sprinkle some cress seeds on top. Follow the instructions below and then place each tub on the windowsill of your classroom. Draw what happens after one week in the boxes below.

wet cotton wool and lid on

wet cotton wool and lid off

dry cotton wool and lid on

dry cotton wool and lid off

Plants need _____ and _____ to grow.

Hallowe'en is coming

Long ago, 1 November was the start of the New Year.
It was also the first day of winter – people called it 'Summer's End'.

They wanted to scare away any ghosts or witches that might come with the winter. They built big bonfires to light up the night. They put on masks and costumes to make themselves look scary. This is how many of our Hallowe'en customs began.

Hallowe'en night

When it begins to get dark, children dress up and go from house to house, looking for treats. They play special games like Bob the Apple and Snap Apple. They may even turn off the lights and tell scary stories! A special fruit cake is made called bairín breac. If you find the ring hidden inside the cake, it means you will get married soon! Watch out!

Talk to older people about what Hallowe'en was like when they were young. Share what you learn with your class. Ask these questions:

1. What games did you play at Hallowe'en? _Snap the Appl_

_____

2. What did you dress up as? _____

_____

3. What is different now about Hallowe'en? _____

_____

4. What remains the same? _____

_____

Your Hallowe'en checklist

Tick the things you do at Hallowe'en.

☐ dress up

☐ go trick or treating

☐ eat bairín breac

☐ carve out a turnip or pumpkin

☐ paint your face

☐ wear a mask

☐ go to a bonfire

☐ play Hallowe'en games

Keeping safe at Hallowe'en

With your class, think of three things you should do to keep safe at Hallowe'en.

1. _____

2. _____

3. _____

Weather

Weather is what happens to the air outside. The air may be hot or cold. This will give us windy, sunny, cloudy or rainy weather. Weather can change as clouds cover the blue sky or the sun comes out.

Everyone is a weather watcher. Why, do you think, people want to know tomorrow's weather forecast? Think about why it is important to farmers, fishermen, sailors, holidaymakers, roadworkers, sportspeople and yourself.

The radio, television and Internet give us information about the weather. Weather reports use symbols that are easy to understand.

Look at the symbols below.

cloudy

cloudy with some sunshine

sunny

Now guess what these symbols mean.

raining

Lighting

Snowing

Look at this map of
Ireland. Choose a weather
symbol for each place.
Draw it in the box.
Write about it below.

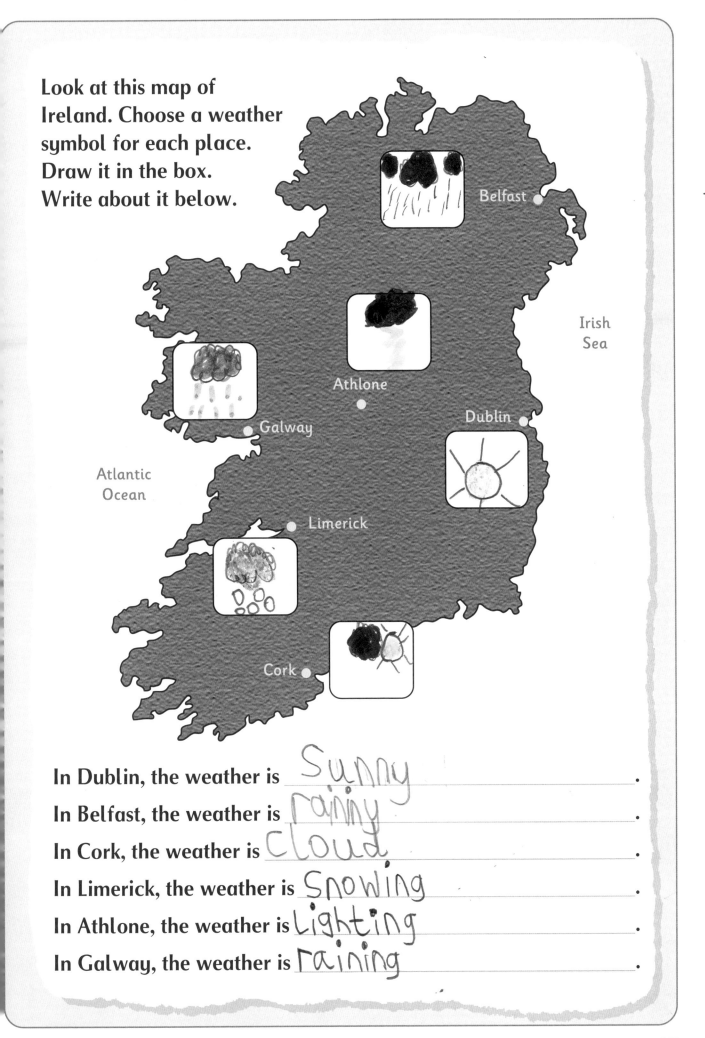

Belfast

Irish
Sea

Athlone

Dublin

Galway

Atlantic
Ocean

Limerick

Cork

In Dublin, the weather is _Sunny_ .
In Belfast, the weather is _rainny_ .
In Cork, the weather is _Cloud_ .
In Limerick, the weather is _Snowing_ .
In Athlone, the weather is _Lighting_ .
In Galway, the weather is _raining_ .

Making new colours

You will need card, scissors, a pencil and crayons or markers.
Cut out five card circles, each about 10 centimetres wide.
Draw a line to divide each circle in half.
On the first circle, colour half blue and half red.
What colour do you think the circle will make when you spin it?
Colour your guess in the chart.
Push a pencil through the middle of the circle. Spin it.
What colour did it make?
Colour in the result.
Try again, using the other colours.

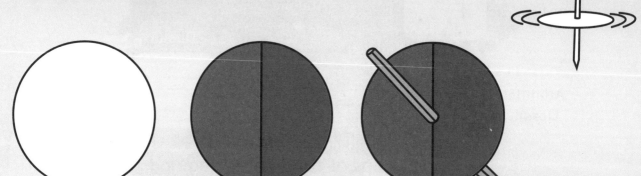

colours used	my guess	colour made

Make your own playdough

Materials needed:

 flour

 salt

 vegetable oil

 tablespoon

 water

 cornflour

 food colouring

 1 cup

 1 bowl

1. Put 2 tablespoons of water, 2 drops of food colouring and 1 tablespoon of salt into the cup. Stir until the salt has dissolved.

2. Put 4 tablespoons of flour, 1 tablespoon of cornflour and 1 tablespoon of vegetable oil into the bowl. Mix well.

3. Add the salty water to the mixture in the bowl. Mix well.

4. Have fun with your playdough!

Cloud cover

Different types of clouds bring different sorts of weather.
You can sometimes tell what the weather will be like by studying
the clouds. Look at the three different types of clouds below
and match each to the correct description.

> **White, fluffy clouds usually mean we will have fine weather.**

> **A blanket of grey cloud, low in the sky, means we might have light rain.**

> **Dark clouds holding lots of water mean we may have stormy weather.**

Light and materials

Light goes through some materials. When this happens, we say the materials are transparent. If light does not go through a material, we say that material is opaque. Think about the materials below and guess whether they are transparent or opaque. Use a torch to test them.

material	my guess		was your guess correct?
	transparent	opaque	✓ or ✗
tea towel			
paper			
glass			
jumper			
frisbee			
plate			
coin			
card			
tissue			
wood			

Brazil

My name is Julio. I live in an apartment in a big city called Rio de Janeiro in Brazil. It is hot all year round. Brazil is the largest country in South America. I speak Portuguese and I am learning English at school. Our summer holidays are in December and January.

My favourite dinner is black beans and rice. There are many people in my city. They build their homes on hillsides, in places called favelas. My city is famous for its carnival.

People celebrate on the streets, dressed in colourful costumes.

samba

carnival

soccer

Brazil nuts

fruits

Amazon

jungle

coffee

beaches

Pelé

Pelé was born in Brazil in 1940. → His parents called him Edson after the famous American scientist Thomas Edison. → His school friends gave him the nickname Pelé.

People say he is the greatest footballer of all time.

European clubs wanted him to play for them. The Brazilian government would not agree – they said he was an official national treasure.

His father loved football and taught him how to play.

He could not afford to buy a football so he practised with a grapefruit or a sock stuffed with newspaper.

He played in four World Cup tournaments and scored many great goals.

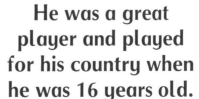

He was a great player and played for his country when he was 16 years old.

Winter

Winter is our coldest season. We need to wear warm clothes to keep the cold out. Sometimes it is so cold that water freezes in pipes, ponds and even rivers. When the air is cold enough, it can snow.

Cold weather makes winter a tough time for birds and animals. Many small animals and insects die in the cold. Farm animals are fed with food the farmer stored in summer and autumn. Sheep stay outdoors and grow a thick, woolly coat to keep warm.

Birds fluff up their feathers to keep the cold out. Finding food can be difficult for birds. We can help them by putting out seeds, bread and fresh water.

During winter, it is dark when we get up for school and again soon after we get home. There is only a little sunshine. Plants need heat from the sun to grow. Many small plants die in the cold. Other plants like trees, shrubs and grasses rest during winter. They will start growing again in spring.

Water and freezing

Water is a liquid. You can pour it. Let's investigate what happens when water and other liquids are frozen.

You will need:

ice cube tray   water   cooking oil

orange juice   vinegar   milk

1. Put some of each liquid into the ice cube tray.
2. Place the tray into a freezer.
3. Think about each liquid. Will it freeze?
   Record your prediction by writing yes or no in that column.
4. After two hours, check what has happened.
   Record your result.

		my prediction	my result
water			
cooking oil			
orange juice			
vinegar			
milk			

Try this experiment.

Put some water into a clear, plastic container.
Add some cooking oil. Leave it for a few minutes.

What happens to the oil? _____

Put the container into the freezer for two hours.
Now what has happened to the oil? _____

The penguin

The penguin is a bird that lives in a very cold place called Antarctica. There is snow and ice there all year round.
Read the penguin's story. Colour the pictures.

I am a penguin. I am a bird, but I cannot fly.

I live in Antarctica.
It is very cold all year round.

Mammy laid my egg. Daddy kept my egg warm on his feet until I hatched.

Mammy looked after me when I hatched from my egg.

Daddy caught fish from the sea for us to eat.

Now I am a great swimmer.
I catch and eat my own fish.

The Titanic

The Titanic was an ocean liner built in Belfast. It was the length of three football pitches.

In April 1912, the liner set off on its first journey with 2228 people on board. At the time, it was the largest moving object ever built.

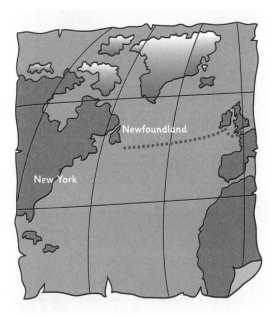

Newfoundland

New York

The Titanic was sailing from England to New York. People thought it was unsinkable.

However, tragedy struck. The Titanic sank, three hours after hitting an iceberg near the island of Newfoundland. Only 705 people survived.

Following a route

A map helps you work out how to get from one place to another.
This is called planning your route. Draw the following routes
on this map, using a different colour for each.

Paul's house to the school (red)   Library to the shop (blue)

Church to the football pitch (green)

Ann's house to the swimming pool (orange)

Which is the longest journey? _____

Which is the shortest journey? _____

Geography

More about routes

Draw a map and mark the route you take when you go from your classroom to the playground.

Draw a map and mark the route you take when you walk from your house to a friend's house.

Making music

Look at the musical instruments below. How do you make sounds with these instruments? Use the word box.

pluck	beat	shake	blow

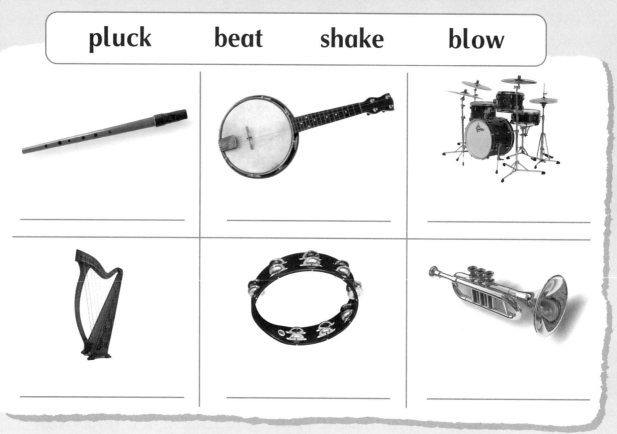

Are these sounds loud or soft?

Properties and uses of materials

Materials have different properties.
Some you can bend, tear, cut or fold.
Some are hard, shiny or heavy.
Materials are chosen to make certain things because of their
properties. For example, metal is a better material than wood
for making knives.

Complete the chart below. The first one is done for you.

material	properties	uses
glass	transparent hard fragile waterproof	windows bottles glasses spectacles
wood		
metal		
plastic		
paper		

CHAT

Schooldays

**Talk about what has changed and what has remained
the same at Fybough National School in County Kerry.**

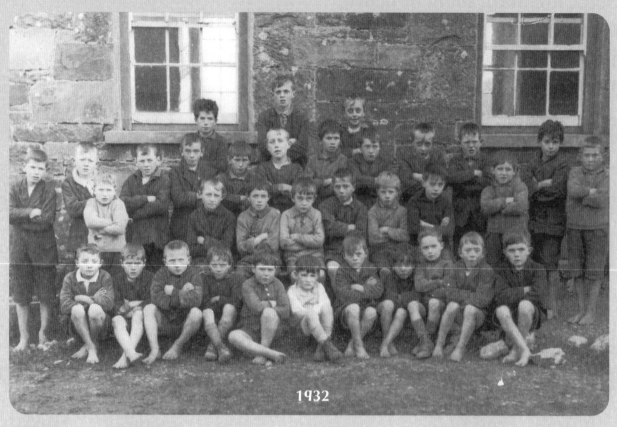
1932

2010

How schools have changed

Interview an older person, maybe a grandparent,
to find out what school was like long ago.

1. What clothes did you wear to school? _____

   _____

2. How many children were in your class? _____

3. What happened at lunchtime? _____

   _____

4. How old were you when you started school? _____

5. What subjects did you learn? _____

   _____

6. How was your classroom heated? _____

   _____

7. What things in your classroom used electricity? _____

   _____

8. What did you use for writing? _____

   _____

9. What was the best thing about school?

   _____

10. What was the worst thing about school?

   _____

Share what you have learned with your class.

Streams, rivers and seas

Most of the Earth is covered by water.
This water is in streams, rivers, lakes, oceans and seas.

A stream is a very small river.
Many streams start in mountains.
Rainwater flows down the mountain and makes streams.
Where the streams join together, they make a river.

A river is water that flows across land.
The water in rivers is not salty. It is called freshwater.
Some rivers flow into lakes.

Most rivers flow into the sea. The place where a river
flows into the sea is called the mouth of the river.

Map of Ireland

This is a map of Ireland.

Ireland is an island because it is surrounded by water.

The longest river in Ireland is the Shannon. It flows through three large lakes on its journey to the sea. It flows into the sea near Limerick. The River Shannon flows through many towns.

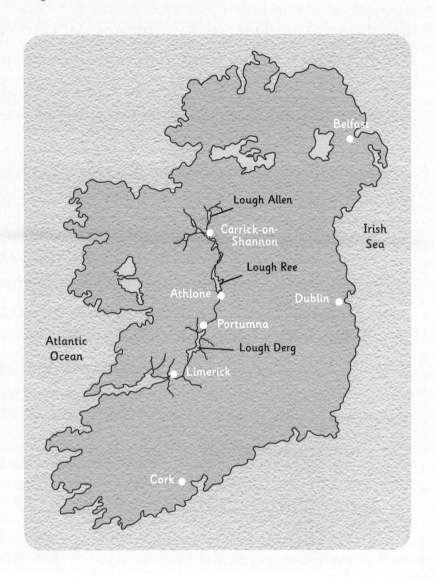

1. Name three lakes on the map.

   (a) _____ (b) _____ (c) _____

2. Name three towns on the map.

   (a) _____ (b) _____ (c) _____

3. Where is the mouth of the River Shannon? _____

4. Name the ocean that the River Shannon flows into. _____

5. Name a river close to your home. _____

The Salmon of Knowledge

Long ago, there was a very famous salmon called the Salmon of Knowledge. It was a huge fish and lived in the River Boyne. People said that the first person to taste this salmon would get great knowledge and see into the future.

Many people came to fish in the river. Each hoped to catch the salmon, but the clever fish always got away.

An old man called Finnegas lived beside the river. He loved poetry, stories and fishing. Every day, he fished for the Salmon of Knowledge. He wanted to be the first person to taste the salmon.

One day, a young man called Fionn came to live with Finnegas. His father had been killed and Fionn was afraid that he too might be killed. Finnegas told him he would be safe with him. They lived happily together. Fionn helped with the cleaning and cooking. At night, they sat around the fire.

Fionn loved listening to poems and stories that Finnegas told. One day, Finnegas rushed back to the hut, carrying a huge fish. He was very excited because he had caught the Salmon of Knowledge!

Fionn lit a large fire and started to cook the fish. Finnegas warned him not to taste it. As the salmon cooked, Fionn noticed a large blister rising on its back.

He pressed the blister with his thumb to burst it. This hurt his thumb, so he put it into his mouth to ease the pain. Something strange happened to Fionn. He could see things that would happen in the future. When Fionn told Finnegas this, Finnegas got angry. 'You must have tasted the fish,' he said. 'I did not,' said Fionn, 'but I burned my thumb and sucked it'. Finnegas was sad because he knew all the salmon's knowledge had been given to Fionn.

Find these fish in the wordsearch.

trout

salmon

cod

haddock

shark

h	e	r	r	i	n	g	h	b	m
v	t	t	r	o	u	t	z	j	a
l	i	b	t	u	n	a	z	d	c
e	y	r	p	l	a	i	c	e	k
e	h	a	d	d	o	c	k	f	e
l	r	q	i	q	z	e	s	n	r
b	c	r	t	s	u	t	h	c	e
r	o	k	t	b	o	p	a	w	l
n	d	a	h	x	d	i	r	a	c
a	s	a	l	m	o	n	k	f	v

herring

tuna

mackerel

eel

plaice

More about weather

Weather is important in our daily lives. It affects the type of homes we build. Around the world, people build different types of houses to suit the way they live, the weather and the building materials that are available.

Some homes in Thailand are built on stilts to keep the houses safe if the land floods.

Morocco is a hot country. The houses are painted white to keep them cool.

Norway is a cold country. The houses have sloping roofs so snow slides off them.

In the deserts of Africa, the Bedouins live in tents. They travel in search of food and water.

Answer these questions:

1. Why do we have gutters and drainpipes on our homes?

_____

2. Would tents make good homes in Ireland? _____

Why? _____

3. Why do houses in Ireland have chimneys?

_____

Earth, moon and sun

Fill in the missing words.

earth

- Earth is a _____.
- It is always on the move.
- _____ is all around it.
- In some places, it is covered with _____, in others with _____.
- If you looked down on it from space, it would look like a blue marble.
- It is your_____.
- Look after it.

water   Air   home   planet   soil

gases   year   light   heat

- The sun is a million times bigger than Earth.
- It gives_____and_____ to Earth.
- It is a star made from hot_____.
- It takes Earth one_____ to travel around the sun.
- Nothing could live on Earth without the sun.

sun

moon

- The moon is a planet.
- It is bare, rocky and dusty.
- It is always _____ there.
- It is Earth's nearest _____.
- Nothing grows or _____ there.
- There is no _____ to breathe.

air   neighbour   dark   lives

Moon-landing

People always wondered what the moon was like. In July 1969,
three American astronauts set off in their spaceship, Apollo 11.
They wanted to be the first astronauts to land on the moon.
Their names were Buzz Aldrin, Michael Collins and Neil Armstrong.
After three days, Apollo 11 reached the moon.
It had a special landing craft called Eagle.
Neil and Buzz landed on the moon in Eagle.
Michael Collins remained behind to look after Apollo 11.
The two astronauts wore special spacesuits because there
is no air to breathe on the moon.

Millions of people watched the moon-landing on television. When Neil Armstrong landed on the moon, he said: 'That's one small step for man, one giant leap for mankind'. The astronauts gathered rocks and dust to bring back to Earth. They also took many photographs. When they returned to Apollo 11, the spaceship began its long journey back to Earth.

They landed safely and were given a hero's welcome. They had become part of history.

1. What could have gone wrong during the journey to the moon?

They cold run

2. Why did the astronauts gather rocks and dust?

To show earth the rocks

3. Why is there no life on the moon?

_____

4. What do you think Neil Armstrong meant when he said: 'That's one small step for man, one giant leap for mankind'?

_____

Ask older people what they remember about the first moon-landing.

Spring

Spring is the season after winter and before summer. It stays brighter for a little longer each day. As the soil gets warmer, many plants begin to grow. Trees are covered with buds. New leaves that have been curled up inside the buds burst out of them. Blossoms grow on many trees. Spring flowers bloom. Many of these grow from bulbs. Bulbs are like stores of food for the plants.

Spring is a good time for animals to have babies. This is because there is now more food to eat. The hibernating animals wake up in spring. They have been sleeping through the cold winter. They are hungry and search for food. Birds are busy building their nests and laying eggs. When the chicks hatch, their parents are kept busy feeding them. When they are big and strong, they leave the nest and fly away. Birds that migrated last autumn return to Ireland again.

In spring, frogs lay frogspawn in ponds and other wet places. Tadpoles hatch from the frogspawn. They grow front and back legs and their tails shrink. Now they are frogs and can live on land and water. They are amphibians.

Science

Spring flowers

Some flowers start to grow in spring.
The days get longer and there is more sunlight.

> tulip   primrose   daffodil   crocus
> snowdrop   hyacinth   violet   bluebell

_____ _____ _____ _____

_____ _____ _____ _____

1. Which is the first flower of spring? _____

2. Name flowers that grow in your area.

_____

_____

3. Which is your favourite? _____

The cuckoo

I am a cuckoo. I return to Ireland from Africa in the spring.

I don't build a nest. I lay my eggs in the nests of other birds.

I pick the nests of birds whose eggs are a similar colour and pattern to mine.

When I lay my egg, I remove an egg from their nest and I fly away. The other birds never know they have been tricked.

When my chick hatches, it pushes all the other eggs and chicks out of the nest. Now it gets all the food and attention.

By the time my chick is ready to leave the nest, it is much bigger than the birds that reared it. They still think this is their baby!

Our feathered friends

Find the birds in the wordsearch.

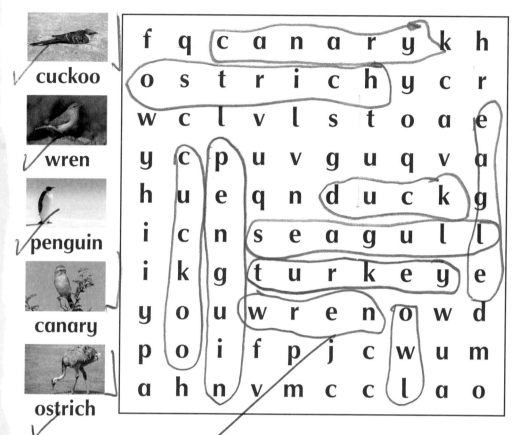

cuckoo

wren

penguin

canary

ostrich

turkey

eagle

seagull

owl

duck

f	q	c	a	n	a	r	y	k	h
o	s	t	r	i	c	h	y	c	r
w	c	l	v	l	s	t	o	a	e
y	c	p	u	v	g	u	q	v	a
h	u	e	q	n	d	u	c	k	g
i	c	n	s	e	a	g	u	l	l
i	k	g	t	u	r	k	e	y	e
y	o	u	w	r	e	n	o	w	d
p	o	i	f	p	j	c	w	u	m
a	h	n	v	m	c	c	l	a	o

Match each bird from the wordsearch to its description below.

eagle	Penguin	Ostrich	cuckoo	owl
a bird of prey	a bird that can't fly	a large bird	a bird that migrates	a nocturnal bird
Wren	dark	Seagull	canary	turkey
a small bird	a bird with webbed feet	a seabird	a pet bird	a bird you can eat

Man-made or natural?

man-made   natural

What do you think these words mean?
Share your ideas with your class.
Now look carefully at these pictures.
Are they man-made or natural?
Write the correct word under each picture.

beach

_____

road

_____

mountain

_____

cave

_____

house

_____

bog

_____

lake

canal

factory

woods

1. What natural features are in your area? _____

_____

2. What man-made features are in your area? _____

_____

3. Name a natural feature in a hot country. _____

_____

4. Name a natural feature in a cold country. _____

_____

Talk about natural features you find in different parts
of the world.

Natural materials

Natural materials are found around us.
They come from plants, animals or the ground. Long ago,
people used natural materials to make everything they needed.
Nowadays, many of the materials we use are man-made.
Man-made materials are natural materials that have been
changed into something new.

Where do the following materials come from?
Put each into the correct box below.

wood   wool   gold   oil   cotton   glass

rubber   clay   feathers   plastic   leather   paper

ground	plants
1. _____	1. _____
2. _____	2. _____
3. _____	3. _____

animals	man-made
1. _____	1. _____
2. _____	2. _____
3. _____	3. _____

Science

A material world

Investigate these objects.

material	sock	cup	ring	ruler	page
What material is it made from?					
Can it be stretched?					
Does it float or sink?					
Does it bend without breaking?					
Is it magnetic?					
Can you cut it?					
Can it be squashed?					
Does it break when dropped?					

A timeline

A timeline tells us the order in which things happen.
Here we have a timeline of the life of a very famous woman called
Florence Nightingale. She lived almost two hundred years ago.

As her parents were rich, Florence was not
expected to work. Instead, she had to lead
the life of a lady, which involved drinking
tea and visiting people. But Florence
wanted to help others. Follow the events
of her life in this timeline.

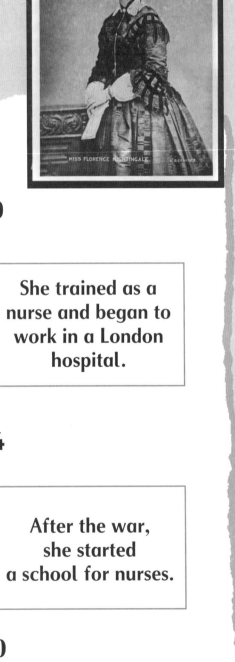

MISS FLORENCE NIGHTINGALE.

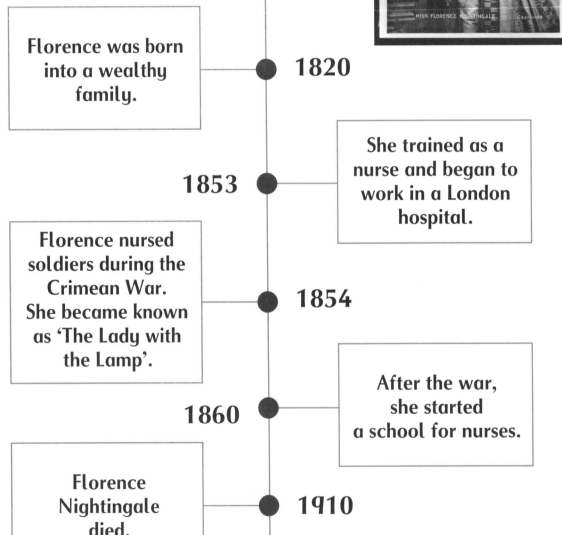

Florence was born into a wealthy family.	**1820**	
	1853	She trained as a nurse and began to work in a London hospital.
Florence nursed soldiers during the Crimean War. She became known as 'The Lady with the Lamp'.	**1854**	
	1860	After the war, she started a school for nurses.
Florence Nightingale died.	**1910**	

My own timeline

Fill in the timeline to show when important things happened in your life.

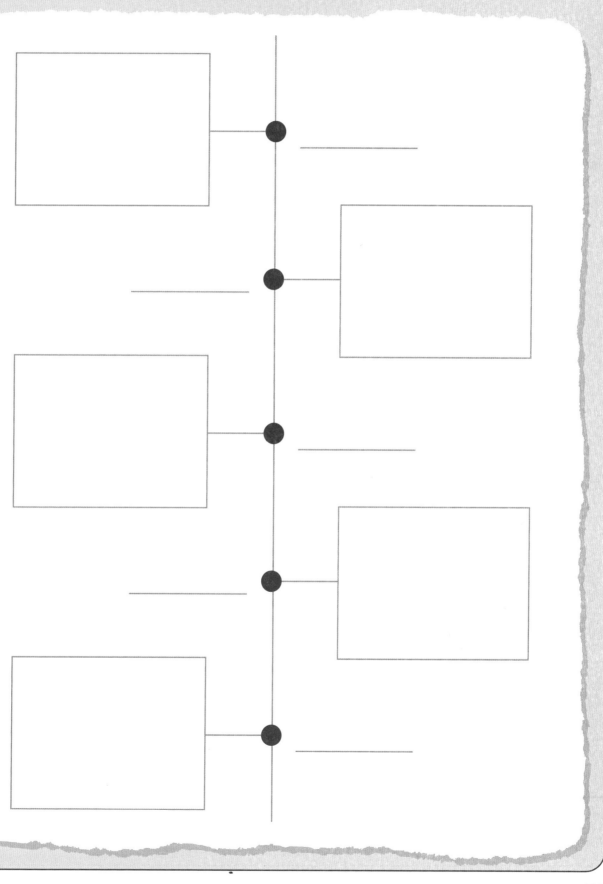

Heat

The sun shines brightly and heats our world in summer.
Heat can change things in different ways. A little heat does not
always change things but a lot of heat usually does.

Try this experiment to discover how heat can change bread.

1. Put two slices of bread on separate plates.

   Are they both the same? _____yes_____

2. Toast one slice.

   How has heat changed the bread? _by the heat_

   Can you change it back again? _No_

3. Now look at the slice of bread and the slice of toast.

   Are they both the same now? _yes_

   Do they smell the same? _yes_

   Do they feel the same? _No_

   Are they the same colour? _No_

   Do they taste the same? _yes_

   Do they sound the same when you bite them? _____

4. Write about what heat can do to:

   (a) chocolate _____

   (b) your skin _____

   (c) a puddle _____

5. What else can heat change?

   (a) ice-cream (b) toys (c) Choclate

Maps

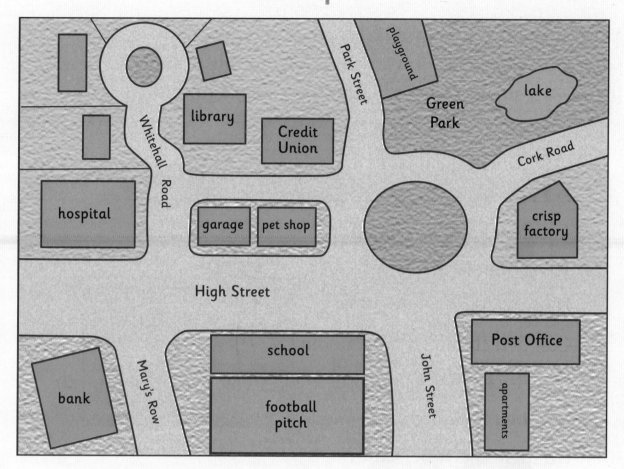

We use maps to find places. The map above is a street map of a small town. The buildings are flat shapes. There are no people or traffic shown on the map.

Use the map to answer these questions.

Which is further from the bank...

1. the Credit Union or the playground? _____

2. the apartments or the school? _____

3. the library or the hospital? _____

Which is nearer to Green Park...

4. the garage or the pet shop? _____

5. the football pitch or the library? _____

6. the crisp factory or the Credit Union? _____

Places of work

Most of us have to work. You work at school.
Grown-ups have jobs to work at. They do this so that
they can provide food and clothes for their families.

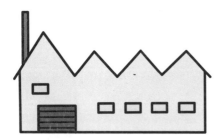

In this factory, people use
machines to make cars.

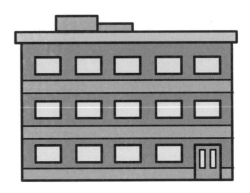

In this office block,
many people work at
desks with computers.

Some people work in shops.
You can often tell what shops
sell by what is in their windows.
What kind of shop is this?

_____

1. Name three jobs people have in your local area.

   (a) _____ (b)_____ (c) _____

2. Name three places in your local area where people work.

   (a) _____ (b)_____ (c) _____

3. Name three shops in your local area.

   (a) _____ (b)_____ (c) _____

Machines – now and then

When your parents, grandparents or older persons were young, could these items be bought? Ask them to help you complete the chart.

machines on sale now	parent could be bought	older person could be bought
electric kettle	Yes	No
microwave	Yes	No
dishwasher	Yes	Yes
mp3 player	No	No
washing machine	Yes	Yes
iron	Yes	Yes
television	Yes	Yes
computer	Yes	No
toaster	Yes	Yes
DVD player	No	No
hairdryer	Yes	Yes
mobile phone	Yes	No

Ask your parent and older person which item they think was the most useful invention and why.

parent dish washer older person Washing machine

Do magnets work through materials?

Paper notes can be stuck to a fridge with a magnet. The paper cannot stop the magnetic force. If the magnetic force is strong enough, it can work through materials as if they were not there.

Try this experiment.
Put a paper clip on a piece of paper.
Can you now move the paper clip by using a magnet held under the paper? Can the magnetic force work through the following objects?
Write yes or no. Predict first and then test.

name of object	my prediction	my result
desk		
copybook		
glass		
plate		
jumper		
book		
ruler		
plastic tray		

Light for life

Green plants need sunlight to live.
They use the light's energy to grow. Plants cannot see light
but they can bend and grow towards where it comes from.
Try this experiment.

You will need:

★ watercress seeds
★ two dishes
★ cotton wool
★ water
★ two cardboard boxes

1. Put a layer of cotton wool in the bottom of each dish.
2. Wet the cotton wool.
3. Sprinkle seeds on the cotton wool.
4. Put the dishes in a sunny windowsill.
5. Cover each dish with a cardboard box.
6. Make a hole in the side of one box.
7. Leave for several days.
8. Check regularly that the cotton wool is damp.

What happened to the seeds in the box with a hole?

_____

_____

What happened to the seeds in the box without a hole?

_____

_____

Past and present

These two photos are of Shop Street in Galway City.
Photo 1 was taken in the 1940s. Photo 2 was taken recently.

1. Why do you think the street has this name?_____

_____

2. What time of the year do you think Photo 2 was taken?

   Give reasons for your answer._____

_____

3. Name three things that have changed on the street.

   (a) _____

   (b) _____

   (c) _____

4. Name three things that have stayed the same.

   (a) _____

   (b) _____

   (c) _____

5. Name two things that have changed in your local area

   since you were born.

   (a) _____

   (b) _____

6. Name two things that have stayed the same.

   (a) _____

   (b) _____

Mapwork

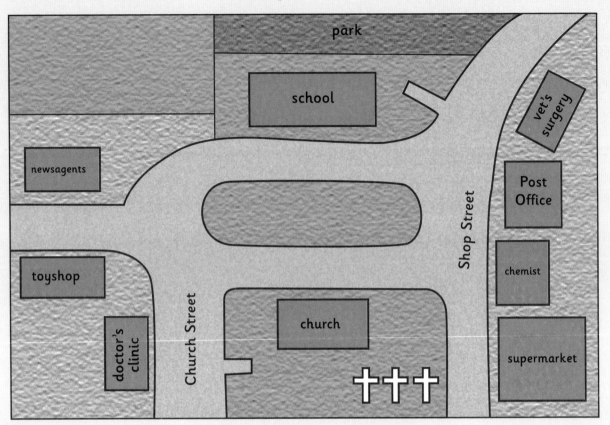

Answer these questions.

1. What is opposite the church? _____

2. What is behind the school? _____

3. Who works next to the Post Office? _____

4. Where is the graveyard? _____

5. What shop is nearest to the doctor's clinic? _____

6. Where would you go to buy stamps? _____

7. Name two things you would buy in a newsagents.

   (a) _____   (b) _____

8. Name four people who would work in this area.

   (a) _____   (b) _____

   (c) _____   (d) _____

Food

We get energy from the food we eat. Our bodies need energy for everything we do. It is important that we have a healthy diet with many different types of food.

There are three main food groups that your body needs. Unscramble the words below to find the names of the different foods in each group.

Some foods help our bodies grow.

gsge	sheece	team	hisf	seban
____	____	____	____	____

Some foods give us vitamins to keep us healthy.

rotrac	palep	clobiroc	reap	ananab
____	____	____	____	____

Some foods give us lots of energy.

ecir	taspa	kasec	topetaos	redab
____	____	____	____	____

Flies

The housefly is a germ-carrying insect.
When this little pest comes into your home, it spreads germs.

A fly has six legs, two wings, two big eyes and two antennae that it uses for smelling.
A fly does not have teeth or a mouth. It squirts juice onto its food. This makes the food soft. The fly then sucks the food through its feeding tube at the front of its head.

FACT

Germs are all around us. They are in the air, on our skin, on animals and on everything we touch. You need a microscope to see them because they are invisible to the naked eye. If harmful germs get into your body, they can make you sick. This is why you should wash your hands after using the toilet and before you eat food.

A fly loves to find uncovered food on which to lay its eggs. After two days, the eggs hatch into maggots. They grow quickly and become too big for their skins. Their old skin falls off and they get a new one. This is called moulting.

After ten days, the maggot turns into a hard case called a cocoon. After another six days, an adult housefly crawls out of the cocoon. It lives for about 21 days. Most flies die when the weather gets cold, but some sleep through the winter.

Files have very interesting feet. They have hooks on them so they can walk upside down on the ceiling or on glass windows. They have taste buds on their feet too. When you see a fly walking on food, it is actually tasting it.

Remember, they don't mind where they put their germy feet – one minute it could be on your bin, the next minute on food left on your worktop.

Now make up some safety rules for keeping food germ-free. The following words will help you:

fridge   pets   cover   food
wash   housefly   hands

_____

_____

_____

_____

_____

_____

Summer

Summer is here now. It is the season after spring and before autumn. Summer is the hottest season of the year. The signs of summer are all around us. Write signs of summer on the rays of sunshine below.

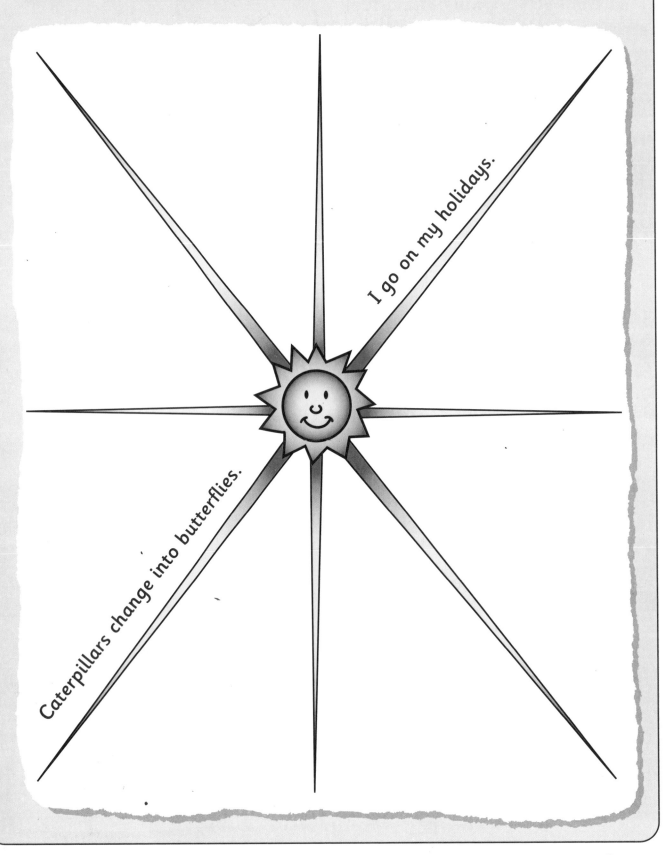

I go on my holidays.

Caterpillars change into butterflies.

Summer fun

Fill in the missing word in each sentence.

> holidays✓   sun✓   butterflies✓
> honey✓   Sandals✓   flowers✓   shines✓

In summer, the sun _Shines_ brightly.

Colourful _flowers_ are in the garden.

Caterpillars change into _butterflies_.

We love to swim on our _holidays_.

Sandals keep our feet cool.

Bees make _honey_ from nectar.

The _Sun_ heats our world.

Summer feelings

I like summer because _there is No School_.

In summer, I look forward to _eating ice-cream_.

In summer, I like looking at _Kites flying in the sky_

I'm glad I'm not a _Sandcastle_ in summer because
I would get washed away by the sea

The worst thing about summer is _It gets too hot_.

In summer, I feel sorry for _My mom and dad_ because
they have to Work while I have School holidays

Four steps to healthy teeth

During your life, you will grow two sets of teeth.
The first set is your baby teeth.
The second set is your adult or permanent teeth.
Your permanent teeth should last a lifetime.

Read the sentences below and draw pictures to show
four steps for healthy teeth.

Eat healthy snacks

Brush properly

Visit your dentist
regularly

Drink milk

Keeping healthy

To keep our bodies healthy, we should eat well, sleep well and get plenty of exercise. You can get exercise by taking part in sport. Name the sports and complete the puzzle.

soccer   skiing   tennis   running
rugby   cycling   swimming

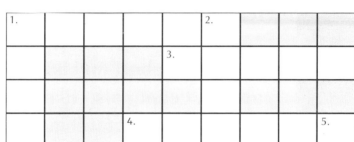

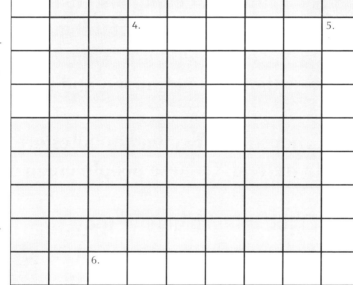

Across
1. There are 11 players on this team.
3. This is played with an oval ball.
4. You need a racket to play this.
6. The equipment you need for this sport has two wheels.

Down
1. This sport takes place on snow.
2. If you are very good at this sport, you might take part in a marathon.
5. This sport takes place in water.

China

More people live in China than in any other country in the world. Beijing is the capital city. It is a very busy and noisy city. There are lots of buses, cars, lorries, bicycles and rickshaws on the streets. People work in shops, factories and offices. Many people live in apartments.

Physical exercise is very important in China. People love to cycle. Sports such as table tennis, volleyball and basketball are popular. People also like T'ai Chi. The gentle movements and breathing exercises help people feel calm. Kung Fu is a popular sport that uses balancing and kicking skills.

Food is eaten using chopsticks. Rice and noodles are always on the menu. Like people in Ireland, Chinese people enjoy drinking tea.

The countryside in China is much quieter than the city. More people live in the country than in the cities. Families live together or very near each other in villages. People work on the land and grow most of their own food. They grow rice, water chestnuts and squash to eat. They buy other foods in markets.

China is famous for many things. It is the home of the Giant Panda. The panda eats bamboo and lives in the wild in China. There are some Giant Pandas in Beijing Zoo.

The Great Wall of China was built 2000 years ago. It was built to keep enemies out.

Many of the things we use every day were invented in China. The Chinese discovered how to make paper, pottery, matches, wheelbarrows, gunpowder and silk.

The most important holiday in China is the Chinese New Year. It is a 15-day celebration. There are lots of parties and fireworks. Children are given presents of money in red envelopes. Each new year is named after an animal. There are 12 animals used to name the years.

Unscramble the words below to name these 12 animals.

odg

ipg

radnog

xo

stoorer

hpees

hsroe

trbabi

ksaen

ymknoe

tra

regti

Silkworm

Silk is a fabric. It is very soft and strong. It is a natural fabric. Did you know that it is spun by silkworms?

The mulberry moth lives in China. It is a white moth with a fat body and small wings. It is unusual because it does not fly or eat. It only lives for five days. During its short life, it lays hundreds of tiny eggs. Silkworm caterpillars hatch from these eggs.

These hungry caterpillars have huge appetites and spend about six weeks eating leaves from the mulberry tree. Then they spin a cocoon around themselves with silk thread. If left alone, an adult moth will hatch from the cocoon after 12 days.

Silk farmers collect cocoons, once they have been been made. They put them into hot water. This makes it easier to unwind the silk threads from the cocoons. The threads are then woven to make silk fabric.

Silk is used to make clothes for special occasions. It is a good fabric to wear in hot countries because it is cool and light. Silk does not shrink when it is washed. It takes about 2000 cocoons to make enough silk for a dress. Silk is not made in Ireland. We buy it from countries like China.

The Legend of the Silkworm

There is a legend in China about how silk was first discovered. In the year 2640BC, the Emperor Huang Ti married Lady Xi Ling Shi. One day, she sat under a mulberry tree to drink some tea. A silk cocoon fell from the tree and landed in her cup. She noticed the delicate threads started to unwind in the hot tea. People say she was the first person to unwind a silk cocoon and use the thread to create silk fabric. Chinese people loved this beautiful fabric. They kept its special secret safe from the rest of the world for 3000 years.

Tell the story of silk. Write a sentence beside each picture.

Chinese writing

In English, we only have to learn 26 letters of the alphabet to be able to read and write. In China, there is no such thing as an alphabet. Instead of learning letters, children learn hundreds of symbols called characters. Each character stands for a word. Look at the examples below.

dog   pig   rabbit

There are also characters for numbers.
Copy each character in the empty boxes.

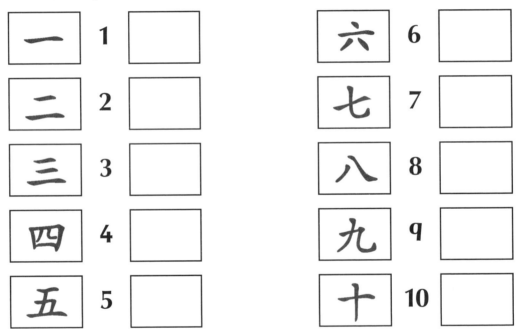

Now write the answers to these sums using Chinese characters.

2 + 5 =   3 + 6 =   5 + 1 =

6 + 4 =   7 − 2 =   10 − 6 =

Soak it up

Some materials soak up liquid. These are absorbent materials.
When a material does not absorb liquid, we say it is waterproof.
Let's test some materials. Remember to predict first.
Pour some water on to a plate. To test each material, place it
in the water. Leave it for a while, then take the material away.

Was it absorbent or waterproof?

material	my prediction		my result	
	absorbent	waterproof	absorbent	waterproof
cotton wool				
cardboard				
plastic				
tinfoil				
kitchen roll				
newspaper				
sponge				

What kind of materials would be good for mopping up spills?

What kind of materials would be good for making umbrellas?

How can you make a difference?

The sun is very important to life on earth. Why?

_____

_____

_____

How do you protect yourself on very sunny days?

_____

_____

_____

How can you help to make our world a better place...

at home?

_____

_____

_____

in your local area?

_____

_____

_____

in school?

_____

_____

_____

Remember!
You can make a difference.

Nature quiz

In each box, draw and name an animal or plant that
fits the description.

grows in a desert	is poisonous	is very strong
has long legs	has a bark	has yellow petals
can be eaten	can sting	lives on land or water
grows from a bulb	has a lovely smell	is extinct

Where in the world...?

Think about places near and far.
Look at a map of the world to help you fill in this chart.
Use words or pictures.

outer
space

me

places
near me

places
further away

places very
far away

Geography